The Enhancement Series • Book Three

THE NEW TESTAMENT

BOOK OF ROMANS

EXPLOSIVELY
ENHANCED

This is an independent work, utilizing the
King James Translation of the Bible, with author
enhancement for clarity and presentation of intended thought.

Robert E. Daley

The Larry Czerwonka Company, LLC
Hilo, Hawai'i

First Edition — November 2014

This book is set in 14-point Garamond

Published by: The Larry Czerwonka Company,
LLChttp://thelarryczerwonkacompany.com

Printed in the United States of America

ISBN:0692330100
ISBN-13: 978-0692330104

All scriptures used in this work are taken from the
King James Version of the Scriptures.

Introduction

The sole purpose for enhancement is for simple clarity.

In this work, the King James Translation of the Bible is unchanged within its textual record. Punctuation and translator added words may be altered, but the sole purpose behind that, is for clearer understanding by the reader.

Since this book is a major doctrinal thesis, it is extremely important that the student of the word of God have a clear cognizance of spiritual truth. Drastic spiritual changes occurred at the resurrection of the New Creation Lord, Jesus Christ of Nazareth. Changes that are largely unknown, or at the least, unrecognized by modern-day Christianity.

This work presents the reality that there are now three separate *types* of Human-Beings in existence, that are now living here on this planet, Earth. These three *types* of Human-Beings are: the **Gentile**, *and the* **Jew**, *and the* **New Creation**.

Failure to understand this reality, will lead to spiritual confusion, and religious insistence. Division will be the result, just as was the case in the scriptural letter that was addressed to the Corinthian church.

This author desires that all Christians become fully aware of who they are now, after having asked Jesus of Nazareth to *save* them, and then direct them by his Holy Spirit, in their walk with God.

THE BOOK OF
ROMANS

CHAPTER 1

1. **Paul,** *of the city of Tarsus,* **a** *willing* **servant of** *the New Creation Lord* **Jesus Christ** *of Nazareth,* **called an apostle** *by Heaven,* *and* **separated** *by the Lord Jesus Christ himself* **unto the gospel of God.**

2. **(Which he,** *that is, God the Father,* **had** *faithfully* **promised afore** *time,* **by his** *appointed* **prophets** *with*in **the Holy Scriptures).**

3. **Concerning his** *Only Begotten* **Son, Jesus Christ our Lord, which was made**, *in his Humanity, even as he had promised,* **of the seed of** *King* **David according to the flesh.**

4. **And** *was* **declared** *to be* **the Son of God, with** *supreme, anointing* **power, according to the** *declaration of the* **Spirit of Holiness, by the** *action of his* **resurrection from the** *spiritual and physical* **dead.**

5. **By whom we**, *who will accept it,* **have received** *the* **grace** *of God,* **and apostleship, for obedience to the faith among all** *of the* **nations, for his name**'*s sake.*

6. **Among whom are ye also** *specifically* <u>**the called**</u> **of Jesus Christ.**

7. **To all** *of the believers* **that be in Rome, beloved of God, called saints** *by Heaven:* **Grace** *be un*to you,

and peace from God our *new heavenly* Father, and *also from* the Lord Jesus Christ, *his Only Begotten Son.*

8.   First *of all*, I thank my God through Jesus Christ *my Lord* for you all, that your *exercise of* faith is spoken of throughout the whole *of the known* world.

9.   For God is my witness, whom I *gladly* serve with my spirit, in the gospel of his Son, that without ceasing I make mention of you *unto our God* always in my prayers.

10.   Making *a* request, if by any *possible* means, now at length, I might have a prosperous journey, by the will of God, to come *also* unto you.

11.   For I long to see you, that I may *be able to* impart unto you some spiritual gift*ings*, to the end *that* ye may be *further* established *in your faith*.

12.   That is, that I may be comforted *within my heart* together with you, by the mutual faith both of you and *of* me.

13.   Now, I would not have you *to be* ignorant, brethren, that oftentimes I purposed to come unto you *before*, (but was let hitherto *and hindered by Satan*,) that I might have some *spiritual* fruit among you also, even as *I have had* among other Gentiles.

14.   *Because of being a New Creature in Christ,* I am *a* debtor both to the Greeks, and to the Barbarians; both to the wise, and to the unwise.

15. So, *with* as much *revelation insight,* as *with*in me *there* is, I am ready to preach the Gospel *of Grace* to you that are at Rome also.

16. For I am not ashamed of the gospel of Christ *Jesus*: for it is the *manifested* power of God unto *the* salvation *of a man's spirit,* to every one that believeth. To the Jew first, *because they are the Chosen People of God, unto whom the Messiah was sent;* and also to the *Gentile* Greek *individual as well.*

17. For there, *with*in *the Gospel of Grace,* is the righteousness of God revealed, from faith to faith. As it is written *within the Scriptures, within the Book of Habakkuk,* "The just shall live by his faith." *(Habakkuk 2:4)*

18. For the *angry, deserved, soon-to-come,* wrath of God is *going to be* revealed from heaven against all ungodliness and unrighteousness of *unredeemed* men, who *continue to* hold the truth *of God* in unrighteousness.

19. Because that *the insight of truth* which may be known of God, is manifest *with*in them, for God hath *already* shewed *it* unto them.

20. For the *reality of the* invisible things *that have come forth* of him, from the creation of the world, are clearly seen *by those individuals that diligently seek him. And those things are* being understood by the things that are made *and are visible,* **even** *having to do* *with* his eternal power and Godhead, so that they are *going to be* without *an* excuse *when the time comes*.

21.   Because that, when they*, in fact,* knew God, they glorified *him* not as *the* God *that he is*, neither were *they* thankful, but became *proud, and* vain in their imaginations, and their foolish heart was darkened.

22.   *Proudly* professing themselves to be *intelligent and* wise, they became fools,

23.   And changed the *pristine* glory of the incorruptible God, *which was manifest in the creation of Adam,* into an image made like *un*to *sinful,* corruptible man, and to *the* birds, and to *the* fourfooted beasts, and *even unto the* creeping things.

24.   Wherefore God also gave them up to *their chosen* uncleanness, *evidenced* through the lusts of their own hearts, to dishonor their own *physical* bodies between themselves.

25.   Who changed the truth of God into a *manifested* lie, and *then* worshipped and served the *created* creature more than *he who is* the Creator, who is blessed for ever. Amen.

26.   For this *very* cause *of free-will choice,* God gave them up unto vile affections. For even their women did change the natural *sexual* use *of their bodies,* into that which is against nature.

27.   And likewise also the men, leaving the natural *sexual* use of the woman*'s body*, burned in their
perverse lust one toward another. Men *sexually interact-
ing* with *other* men, working that which is *unnatural
and* unseemly, and receiving *with*in themselves that
justifiable recompense of their error which was meet
and deserving.

28.   And even as they *have rebelled, and* did not like
to retain God *with*in **their** knowledge, God *responded,
and* gave them over to a reprobate *thinking* mind, to
do those things which are not convenient.

29.   Being filled with all unrighteousness, *and*
covetousness, *and* maliciousness. *Being* full of envy,
murder, debate, deceit, *and* malignity. *They are*
whisperers,

30.   *And* backbiters, *willing* haters of God. De-
spiteful, proud, boasters, inventors of evil things,
and disobedient to *their* parents.

31.   Without *spiritual* understanding *or even interest.
Unstable* covenantbreakers *are they*. Without *any* natural affection, implacable, *and* unmerciful.

32.   Who knowing *of* the *righteous* judgment of
God, that they which *willingly* commit such *vile*
things are *indeed* worthy of death, not only do the
same *vile things*, but *they also* have pleasure in *all of*
them that do them.

CHAPTER 2

1.   Therefore, thou art inexcusable, O *sinful and unconverted Gentile or Jewish* man, whosoever thou art *amongst unredeemed Mankind,* that judgest *what another sinful man doest.* For wherein thou judgest another *sinful man,* thou condemnest thyself. For thou *thyself, O sinful and unconverted Gentile or Jewish man,* that judgest *another sinful man,* doest the *very* same things. *Not that the New Creation Human-Beings are exempt from judgment before the Bema Seat of Christ, by any means. But right now, we are not observing the recreated, supernatural, New Creation Human-Beings, but the unconverted, unredeemed, natural Jewish and Gentile individuals.*

2.   But we are *certain, and are* sure that the judgment *that cometh forth* of *the living* God, is according to *the* truth, against *all of* them which commit such *vile* things.

3.   And thinkest thou this, O *sinful* man, that judgest them which do such things, and *then turnest right around, and* doest the same *things*; that thou shalt escape the judgment *that is going to come forth* of God?

4.   Or despisest thou the riches of his goodness *and grace,* and forebearance and longsuffering? Not knowing that *it is* the goodness of *a loving* God, *and not his wrath, that* leadeth thee to repentance.

5. But *thou shalt be judged* **after thy** *sin affected, and* **hardness and impenitent,** *condition of thy* **heart, treasurest up unto thyself** *deserved* **wrath against the day of wrath, and** *the* **revelation of the righteous judgment of God.**

6. **Who**, *during the Millennial Reign of Christ, and particularly at the Great White Throne judgment,* **will render to every** *single, unredeemed* **man** *on this earth,* **according to his** *personal* **deeds.**

7. **Unto them,** *during the Millennial Reign of Christ,* **who by patient continuance in** *good behavioral* **well doing,** *who were* **seek***ing* **for glory and honour and immortality;** *they shall enter into* **Eternal Life.**

8. **But unto them that are** *naturally* **contentious, and do not obey the truth** *contained within the word of God,* **but** *rather* **obey** *sin and* **unrighteousness;** *they shall suffer* **indignation and** *the* **wrath** *of God.*

9. **Tribulation and anguish,** *shall come* **upon every soul of** *unredeemed* **man that doeth evil; of the** *natural* **Jew***ish man* **first,** *because of covenant ramifications,* **and** *then* **also of the** *natural unconverted* **Gentile.**

10. **But glory,** *and* **honour, and peace,** *shall be ministered* **to every** *unconverted, natural* **man that worketh good** *during the Millennial Reign of Christ.* **To the** *unredeemed, natural* **Jew***ish man* **first,** *because of covenant ramifications,* **and** *then* **also to the** *unconverted, natural* **Gentile man.**

11.   For there is no respect*ing* of persons with God.

12.   For as many *unconverted, natural men* as have sinned without *having the privilege of the* **Law** *of Moses, (that is, all Gentile-nation individuals). They* **shall also perish without** *the* **Law** *of Moses.* **And as many** *unconverted, natural men* **as have sinned** *and disobeyed God with*in the **Law** *of Moses, (that is, all Jewish individuals), they* **shall be judged by the Law** *of Moses.*

13.   (For *during the days in which we now live,* not *simply* the hearers of the **Law** *of Moses* **are** *considered* just*ified* before God, but *only* the doers of the **Law** *of Moses* shall be justified.

14.   For when the *unconverted, natural* **Gentiles,** which have not the **Law** *of Moses,* do by nature the things contained *with*in the **Law** *of Moses,* these having not the **Law** *of Moses, to actively guide them,* are *become* a law unto themselves.

15.   Which shew the *actual* work*ing* of the **Law** *of Moses* written *with*in their hearts. **Their** *own* conscience also bearing *them* witness. And *their own* thoughts the mean while accusing or else excusing one another *as sinful men do.*) *However, no flesh shall be justified by the works of the Law of Moses, because Jesus Christ of Nazareth is "the way, and the truth, and the life, and no man cometh unto the Father except through him." (John 14:6)*

16. In the *prophesied* day, *is* when God shall judge the secrets of men*'s hearts* by Jesus Christ according to my gospel.

17. Behold, thou art *called* a Jew*ish person, in the natural,* and restest in the *safety of* the Law *of Moses,* and makest thy boast of *being in covenant with* God?

18. And *say that thou* knowest *his* will, and *proceed to* approve*th* the things that are more excellent, being instructed out of the Law *of Moses.*

19. And art confident that thou thyself art a guide of the *Gentiles,* who are *spiritually* blind; *and* a light of them which are *walking* in darkness.

20. An instructor of the foolish, *and* a teacher of babes, which hast the form of knowledge and of the truth in the Law *of Moses.*

21. Thou therefore which teachest another *concerning proper righteous behavior,* teachest thou not thyself? Thou that preaches *unto others that* a man should not steal, dost thou steal?

22. Thou that sayest *that* a man should not commit adultery, dost thou commit adultery *thyself?* Thou that *sayest that thou* abhorrest idols, dost thou *err and* commit sacrilege?

23. Thou that makest thy boast of *having confidence in* the Law *of Moses,* through *the* breaking *of* the Law *of Moses* dishonourest thou God?

24.   For the name of God is blasphemed among the Gentiles through you, *and your behaviour,* as it is written.

25.   For *covenant* circumcision verily profiteth *thou,* if thou *be a* keep*er of* the *whole of the* Law *of Moses.* But if thou be*come* a breaker of the Law *of Moses, in any point,* thy *covenant* circumcision is made *unprofitable, just as if thou wast an individual of* uncircumcision.

26.   Therefore, if the *Gentile* uncircumcision *person* keep*eth* the *behavioral* righteousness of the Law *of Moses,* shall not his *position of* uncircumcision *become just as profitable as your position, and shall be* counted for circumcision?

27.   And shall not *the physical* uncircumcision which is *produced* by nature, if it *shall* fulfil the Law *of Moses, ultimately* judge thee, who by the *very* letter and *physical* circumcision dost transgress the Law?

28.   For, *in God's eyes,* he is not a Jew, which is one *only* outwardly. Neither *is that physical* circumcision, which is outward in the flesh.

29.   But he *is considered* a Jew, which is one inwardly; and *his* circumcision *is not only that which is in the flesh, but more importantly, that* which is of the heart, in the spirit, *and* not *simply* in the letter; whose praise *is* not of men, but of God.

CHAPTER 3

1.　　What advantage then *within this world*, hath the Jew*ish man*? Or what *beneficial* profit *is there in being a member* of *covenant* circumcision?

2.　　Much every way! Chiefly, because that unto them were committed the *very* oracles of God *for safe keeping. Oracles which grant unto the Abrahamic Covenant people of God, a law for behavioral modification, which is set forth as a schoolmaster. And in addition, declaration of all things that pertain to life and godliness, that no man might be able to stand before God, at the time of judgment, with any plausible excuse.*

3.　　For what if some *Jewish covenant men* did not believe *what God did within the prophetical finished work of Christ Jesus upon the cross*? Shall their *willful* unbelief make the faith of God without effect?

4.　　God forbid! Yea, let God be true, *in what he says and does*, but every man a liar. As it is written *within Psalm 51*, "That thou mightest be justified in thy sayings, and mightest overcome when thou art judged." *(Psalms 51:4)*

5.　　But if our *behavioral* unrighteousness *contradicts, and yet* commend*s*, the *very* righteousness of God, what shall we say? Is God unrighteous who taketh *justified* vengeance *upon a person*? (I speak as a man)

6.   God forbid! For then how shall God judge the *whole* world, *if he hath not put forth a standard for men to live by*?

7.   For if the truth of God, *which is contained within his word,* hath more abounded through my lie unto his glory, why yet am I also *ultimately* judged as a sinner?

8.   And not *rather,* (as we be slanderously reported, and as some affirm that we say,) Let us do evil, that good may come? Whose damnation is just*ified.*

9.   What then? Are we, *as Jews, any* better *than they*? No, in no wise! For we have before proved *that* both *natural, unconverted* Jews and *natural, unconverted* Gentiles, that they are all under *the power of* sin.

10.   As it is written *in Psalm 14,* "There is none righteous, no, not one.

11.   There is none that understandeth, there is none that seeketh after God." *(Psalms 14:2-3)*

12.   "They are all gone out of the way," *according to the prophet Isaiah,* "they are together become unprofitable; there is none that doeth good, no, not one." *(Isaiah 53:6)*

13.   "There throat is an open sepulcher." *(Psalms 5:9)* "With their tongues they have used deceit; *and* the poison of asps *is* under their lips." *(Psalms 140:3)*

14.   "Whose mouth *is* full of cursing and bitterness." *(Psalms 10:7)*

15.   "*And* their feet *are* swift to shed blood." *(Proverbs 1:16)*

16.   "Destruction and misery *are* in their ways;

17.   And the way of peace have they not known." *(Isaiah 59:7-8)*

18.   "There is no fear of God before their eyes." *(Psalms 36:1)*

19.   Now we *have come to learn, and* know that what things soever the Law *of Moses* saith, it saith *firstly* to them who are *living directly* under the Law *of Moses within the covenant parameters: that is, the unconverted Jewish individuals. But in addition,* that every mouth may be stopped *from their flagrant excuses,* and *because of that stated Law,* all *of* the world may become guilty before God *when the time of judgment comes.*

20.   Therefore, *we should understand, that* by the deeds of the Law *of Moses* there shall no flesh be *able to be* justified *(or declared "not guilty")* in his sight. For by the *giving of the* Law *of Moses, (as a behavior modifier, to the Jewish covenant people only),* is the knowledge of sin *and its operation, made clear to the entire world.*

21.   But now, *since the impacting resurrection of Jesus Christ, is* the *true* righteousness of God, *which is actually found within the very personage of Christ Jesus himself,* established. Without *the need for* the Law *of Moses, that righteousness* is manifested *today,* being witnessed by

the *very* law and the *writings of the* prophets *that it replaces.*

22.   Even the *gifted* righteousness of God *which is* by *the* faith of Jesus Christ, unto all *Human-Beings* and upon all *of* them that believe *unto that righteousness.* For there is no difference *between the natural, unconverted Gentile or the natural, unconverted Jew.*

23.   For all *Human-Beings* have sinned, and come short of the glory of God.

24.   Being justified, *and declared "not guilty"* freely, by his grace *only*, through the *finished* redemption *work* that is in Christ Jesus.

25.   Whom God hath set forth *to be* a *substitute and a* propitiation through *exercised* faith in his *shed* blood. To declare his righteousness for the remission of *the* sins that are past, through the forbearance *and graciousness* of God.

26.   To declare, *I say*, at this time his, *that is, God's* righteousness: that he might be just *in his judgments*, and the justifier of him which believeth in Jesus.

27.   Where is boasting then *on the behalf of men*? It is excluded. By what law? *The law* of works? Nay: but by the Law of Faith.

28.   Therefore, we conclude that a*n unredeemed* man is justified, *and declared "not guilty"*, by *the power of*

faith, **without** *having the necessary requirements of perform-ing* **the deeds of the Law** *of Moses.*

29. *Is he* **the** *One True* **God of the Jews only?** *Is he* **not also** *the One True God* **of the Gentiles** *as well?* **Yes, of the Gentiles also.**

30. **Seeing** *that it is* **one God, which shall justify the** *natural, unconverted Jewish* **circumcision by** *the* **faith** *which they were to have developed . . . and when the time came . . . to have transferred to the finished work of Christ, having had the schoolmaster.* **And,** *the natural, unconverted Gentile* **un-circumcision through** *the* **faith** *that they were to exercise in also accepting the finished work of what Christ did on the cross.*

31. **Do we then make void the Law** *of Moses* **through faith? God forbid! Yea, we establish the Law** *of Moses as being valid for the purpose for which it was brought forth.*

CHAPTER 4

1. **What shall we say then, that Abraham our father, as pertaining to the** *works of the* **flesh, hath found?**

2. **For if Abraham were justified by** *his* **works** *of the flesh,* **he hath** *reason* **whereof to glory; but not be-fore God.**

3.   For what saith the Scripture? "Abraham believed *what* God *had said*, and it was *ac*counted unto
him for righteousness." *(Genesis 15:6)*

4.   Now to him that worketh *for something,* is the
recompense and **reward** *that he receives* not reckoned of
the free **grace** *of unmerited favor*, but *because* of *a* **debt** *that
is owed by the one that he worked for.*

5.   But to him that worketh not, but *simply* believeth on him that *is able to* justifieth the ungodly,
his faith is *what is* counted for righteousness.

6.   Even as David also describeth the blessedness of the man, unto whom God *will* imputeth
righteousness without *the* works *of the flesh.*

7.   *Saying,* "Blessed *are* they whose iniquities
are forgiven, and whose sins are covered.

8.   Blessed *is* the man to whom the Lord will
not impute sin." *(Psalms 32:1-2)*

9.   *Cometh* this blessedness then upon the *natural, unconverted Jewish* circumcision *people* **only,** or
upon the *natural, unconverted people of the* uncircumcision also? For we say, *from Scriptural declaration,* that
his faith was reckoned to Abraham for righteousness.

10.   How was it then reckoned? When he was in
natural, unconverted Jewish covenant circumcision, or *when
he was still a rank heathen* in *natural, unconverted* uncircumcision? Not in *natural, unconverted Jewish covenant*

circumcision, but *while he was yet* **in** *natural, unconverted* uncircumcision.

11.   And he received the *covenant* sign of circumcision *when the covenant was ratified*, *which was* a *confirming* seal of the righteousness of the faith which *he had exercised*, *yet* being uncircumcised. That he might be*come* the father of all *of* them that *simply* believe, though they be not *among those who are covenantly* circumcised. That *the* righteousness *of* God might be imputed unto them also.

12.   And the father of circumcision to them who are not of the *natural, unconverted Jewish covenant* circumcision only, but who also walk in the *same* steps of that faith of our father Abraham, which *he had* being *yet a rank heathen, and an unconverted, uncircumcised idolater*.

13.   For the promise, that *he* should be the heir of the world, was not *made directly un*to Abraham, or to his *natural* seed, through the Law *of Moses*, but *rather the seed that would emerge* through the righteousness of faith.

14.   For if they which are of the Law *of Moses* **be** *the* heirs *of righteousness, then the exercise of* faith is made void, and the *inheritance* promise *that was* made of none effect.

15.   Because the Law *of Moses* worketh wrath. For where no *active* Law *of Moses* is *in operation*, **there** *is* no *imputed* transgression.

16.   Therefore, *concerning the promise,* it is of faith, that *it might* be by *the extended* grace *of God*. To the end *that* the promise might be sure to all *of* the seed. Not to that *natural, unconverted Jewish circumcision* only, which is of the Law *of Moses*, but to that *group of natural, unconverted individuals* also which is of the faith of Abraham, who is the father of us all *who believe*.

17.   (As it is written, "I have made thee a father of many nations." *(Genesis 17:4-5)*) Before him whom he believed, *even* God, who quickeneth *and maketh alive* the dead, and calleth *all of* those things which be not, as though they were.

18.   Who against hope, *because of his age,* believed in hope, that he might become the father of many nations, according to that which was spoken, "So shall thy seed be." *(Genesis 15:5)*

19.   And being not weak in faith, he considered not his own body now *all but* dead, when he was about an hundred years old, neither yet the *nonproductive* deadness of Sarah's womb.

20.   He staggered not at the *inheritance* promise of God through unbelief; but was strong in *his* faith, giving glory to God.

21.　　And being fully persuaded that, what he has promised, he was able also to perform.

22.　　And therefore it was imputed *unto* him *by God* for righteousness *sake.*

23.　　Now it was not *only* written for his sake alone that it was imputed to him.

24.　　But for us also, to whom it shall be imputed, if we *also* believe on him that raised up Jesus our Lord from the *spiritual and physical* dead.

25.　　Who was delivered *unto death* for our offences, and was raised again *unto New Life* for our justification.

CHAPTER 5

1.　　Therefore being justified *and declared not guilty* by faith, we have *obtained* peace with God *the Creator,* through our Lord Jesus Christ, *who is our mediator.*

2.　　By whom also we have *received* access, by faith, into this *unmerited* grace wherein we stand, and rejoice in hope of the glory of God *that is to come.*

3.　　And not only so, *as we have just stated,* but we glory in tribulations also: knowing that tribulation *will* worketh patience *within us;*

4.　　And patience, *will produce* experience; and experience, *will gender* hope;

5.   And hope *will* maketh *us to* not *be* ashamed. Because the love of *our* God is shed abroad in our hearts by the Holy Ghost which is *freely* given unto us.

6.   For when we were yet without *any spiritual* strength*, as sinners,* in due time Christ died for the ungodly.

7.   For scarcely for a righteous man will one *purpose to* die: yet peradventure for a good man some would even dare to die.

8.   But God commendeth his love toward us, in that, while we were yet sinners, Christ *came forth and* died for us.

9.   Much more then, being now justified by his *shed* blood, we shall be saved from *the* wrath *of a just God* through him.

10.   For if, when we were *yet* enemies, we were reconciled to *the One True* God by the death of his *Only Begotten* Son, much more, being *then* reconciled, we shall be saved *from wrath and from eternal destruction,* by his *New* Life.

11.   And not only *so as we have said,* but we also re*joice* in God through our Lord Jesus Christ, by whom we have now received the *blood* atonement *of not just covering our sins, but in remitting them altogether.*

12.   Wherefore, as by one man*, named Adam,* sin entered into the world *for a second time,* and *spiritual and physical* death *came* by sin; and so *spiritual* death passed upon all men, for that all have sinned *and come short of the glory of God.*

13.　(For until the Law *of Moses came forth,* sin was *still* in the world: but sin is not imputed when there is no law *to make it known for what it is.*

14.　Nevertheless, *spiritual and physical* death *still* reigned from Adam to Moses, even over them that had not sinned *in the same way, and* after the similitude of Adam's transgression, who is the figure *and shadow* of him that was to come, *that is, Jesus Christ our Lord.*

15.　But not as the offence, so also *is* the free gift: for if through the offence of *only* one *man,* named *Adam,* many *men and women* be*come* dead, much more the grace of God, and the gift by *that* grace, **which is** by *only* one man, Jesus Christ, hath abounded unto many *men and women, unto eternal life.*

16.　And not as *sweeping as* **it was** by *the* one that *had* sinned, **so is** the gift *of redemption available for all those who will receive it.* For the judgment *that came forth because of sin,* **was** by one *man un*to condemnation *for all*; but the free gift *that came by one man,* **is** of many offences *being forgiven, for all men and women who will receive it,* unto justification, *and the declaration of "not guilty", by reason of grace.*

17.　For if by one man's offence *spiritual and physical* death reigned *over all* by one; much more they which *will* receive *the* abundance of grace, *by a forgiving God,* and of the *free* gift of *legal* righteousness, shall reign in *this* life by one, Jesus Christ.)

18.   Therefore, as by the offence of *only* one *man, judgment came* upon all *other* men to condemnation. Even so, by the righteousness of *only* one *man, named Jesus Christ of Nazareth,* **the free gift** *of redemption came* upon all men, *that would receive it,* unto *declared* justification of *New* Life.

19.   For as by one man's disobedience, many were made sinners, so by the obedience of one *man,* shall *as* many be made righteous *who will receive it.*

20.   Moreover the Law *of Moses* entered, *as a behavior modifier,* that the offence might abound. But *we have seen by his mercy, that* where sin *hath* abounded, *so* grace did much more abound.

21.   That as *the power of* sin hath reigned, *even* unto death, even so might *extended* grace reign through *demonstrated* righteousness, *ultimately* unto Eternal Life, by Jesus Christ our Lord.

CHAPTER 6

1.   What shall we say then? Shall we continue *to live* in sin, *so* that *the* grace *of a loving God* may abound?

2.   God forbid! How shall we that are *now* dead to sin, *because of the shed blood sacrifice of Christ Jesus*, live any longer *in the vileness* therein?

3.   Know ye not, that so many of us as were baptized into *the body of* Jesus Christ were*, in reality,* baptized into his *spiritual* death?

4.   Therefore we are buried with him by *that* baptism into *spiritual* death: that like as Christ was raised up from the *spiritual* dead, by the glory of the Father, even so we also should *now* walk in *the* newness of *spiritual* life *through the New Birth.*

5.   For if we have been planted together in the likeness of his *spiritual* death, we shall be also *raised up* **in the likeness** of **his** *spiritual* resurrection *unto New Life. And now, because of his spiritual birth from death unto life, we are able to become Born-Again within our spirits, by trusting in what he did for us.*

6.   Knowing this, that *when the New-Birth of our spirit occurs,* our old man is crucified with *him,* that the body of *actively operating* sin might be destroyed, *and* that henceforth we should not serve sin *anymore.*

7.   For he that is *crucified, and* dead *unto himself and the dictates of his flesh,* is freed from *the power and obligation of* sin.

8.   Now if we *legally* be dead with Christ, we *purpose to* believe that we shall *now* also *spiritually* live *and reign* with him.

9.   Knowing *in our knower* that Christ being raised *up* from the dead . . . *that he* dieth no more *spiritually or physically*. Death, *in any of its conditions*, hath *absolutely* no more dominion over him *ever again*.

10.   For in that he *spiritually and physically really* died, he died unto *the power and demands of* sin *just* once. But in that he *now* liveth *again*, he liveth *wholly* unto God.

11.   Likewise *then*, reckon ye also yourselves to be dead indeed unto sin, but *now spiritually* alive unto God through *the finished work of* Jesus Christ our Lord.

12.   Let not sin therefore, *by any means*, reign in your mortal body, that ye should obey it in the lusts thereof *of the flesh*.

13.   Neither yield ye your *individual bodily* members *as* instruments of unrighteousness *in giving in* unto sin. But *instead*, yield yourselves unto *the leading of the Spirit of* God, as those that are *indeed* alive from the *condition of being spiritually* dead. And *yield* your *bodily* members *as* instruments of righteousness unto God.

14.   For sin shall not have *any legal* dominion over you. For ye are not under the *dictates of the* Law *of*

Moses any more; but *ye are* under *the wonderful abundance of the blanket of God's merciful* grace.

15.   What then? Shall we *continue to willfully* sin, because we are not under the *dictates of the* Law *of Moses any more*, but under *unmerited* grace? God forbid!

16.   Know ye not, that to whom ye *choose to* yield yourselves *as* servants to *willingly* obey, his servants ye *truly* are to whom ye *willingly* obey; whether of *the dictates and power of* sin unto *certain* death, or of *chosen* obedience unto righteousness *and true holiness?*

17.   But *the* God *of mercy* be thanked, that ye were, *when ye were in your old man,* the servants of sin, but ye have *willingly* obeyed from the *very* heart, that form of *Biblical redemption* doctrine which was delivered *unto* you.

18.   *And,* being then made free from *the power of* sin, ye became the servants of righteousness, *and children of the Most High God.*

19.   I speak after the manner of men because of the infirmity of your flesh. For as ye have yielded your *bodily* members *as* servants to uncleanness *in days gone by,* and *unto submission to* iniquity, unto *further continuing* iniquity; even so now *that ye are Born-Again,* yield your *bodily* members *as* servants to righteousness unto holiness.

20.   For when ye were the servants of sin, ye were free from *any spiritual requirements of* righteousness.

21.   *Tell me,* what fruit had ye then, in those things whereof *today* ye are now ashamed? For the end of those things is *certain spiritual* death.

22.   But now, being made free from *the dictates and power of* sin, and *truly* becom*ing* servants *un*to *the living* God, ye have your *righteous* fruit unto holiness, and the end *of the matter being,* Everlasting Life.

23.   For the wages, *or payment for, or compensation* of sin *is surely* death; but the *free* gift of God *is granted* Eternal Life through Jesus Christ our Lord.

CHAPTER 7

1.   Know ye not, brethren, (for I speak to them that *think that they* know *what* the Law *of Moses declares,*) how that the Law *of Moses* hath *absolute* dominion over a*ny Abrahamic Covenant* man *for* as long as he *physically* liveth *on this earth?*

2.   For the *Abrahamic Covenant* woman which hath an *Abrahamic Covenant* husband, is *totally and completely* bound by the Law *of Moses* to her husband so long as he *physically* liveth. But if the husband be *physically* dead, she is *then* loosed from the *binding* Law of Husband.

3.   So then if, while *her* husband *physically* liveth, she *leaveth him and shall* be married to another man, she shall be called, *by the Law of Moses,* an adulteress. But if her husband be *physically* dead, she is free from that *binding* Law *of Husband*; so that she is, *in reality,* no adulteress, *even* though she be married to another man.

4.   Wherefore, my brethren, *this truth is an allegory of our coming to Christ. With the New-Birth,* ye also are *now* become dead to the Law *of Moses,* by *your becoming part of* the Body of Christ. That ye should be *covenantly* married to another, even to him who is raised *up* from the dead, *for the purpose* that we should bring forth fruit unto *life, and unto* God.

5.   For when we were *unconverted, and carnal* in the flesh, the *actions and* motions of sins, which were *pointed out* by the Law *of Moses,* did work *with*in our *bodily* members to bring forth fruit unto death.

6.   But now, *being in Christ,* we are delivered from the Law *of Moses,* that *once* being *spiritually* dead wherein we were held *by that Law*; that *now* we should serve *our* God in *the* newness of spirit *life,* and not *continue in* the oldness of the letter *of what the Law of Moses declares.*

7.   What shall we say then *to this reality*? *Is* the Law *of Moses really* sin? God forbid! Nay, I had not known *about* sin, but by the Law *of Moses.* For I had

not known *about* lust, except the Law *of Moses* had said, "Thou shalt not covet." *(Exodus 20:17)*

8.　　But *the Law of* Sin, taking occasion by the *holy* commandment, wrought in me all manner of *death issues, through* concupiscence. For without the Law *of Moses being on the scene,* sin *effectually* **was** dead.

9.　　For I was *seemingly* alive without the Law *of Moses* once *upon a time.* But when the *holy* commandment came *forth,* *it revealed sin for what it really was, and then* sin revived, and I died.

10.　　And the *holy* commandment, which **was** *originally* **ordained** to *reveal* life, I found to be unto death *for me.*

11.　　For *the active operation of* sin, taking occasion by the *holy* commandment, *dictated to, and* deceived me, and *then* by it slew *me.*

12.　　Wherefore the Law *of Moses* is holy, and the commandment *is* holy, and just, and good.

13.　　Was then that which is *holy and* good made death unto me? God forbid! But *the Law of* Sin *is the culprit,* that it might appear *to be* sin *by the revelation of the Law of Moses.* **Working death in me by** *utilizing* that which is *holy and* good. That *the Law of* Sin, by the *holy* commandment, might *truly be seen for what it is, and then* become exceeding sinful.

14.　　For we *should* know that the Law *of Moses* is *really* spiritual. But *in my spiritually dead condition,* I am carnal *and natural*, **sold** *into bondage by Adam, and des-tined to live and operate* **under** *the Law of* **Sin** *forever.*

15. **For that which I do**, *I protest and declare that* **I allow not. For what I** *declare that I* **would** *want to do*, **that do I not. But what I** *profess that I* **hate, that do I.**

16. **If then I** *actually* **do that which I** *declare that I* **would not, I consent unto the Law** *of Moses, by my actions,* **that** *it is* **good** *and holy.*

17. **Now then,** *it must be recognized, that in my spiritu-ally dead condition,* **it is no more I that do it, but** *the power and dictates of the Law of* **Sin, that** *continues to* **dwelleth in me.**

18. **For I know that in** *the unredeemed* **me (that is, in my** *natural* **flesh,) dwelleth no good thing. For to** *freely* **will** *to do good* **is** *indeed* **present with me; but** *how* **to** *actually* **perform that which is good I find not.**

19. **For the good that I** *declare that I* **would** *want to do*, **I do not. But the evil which I** *proclaim that I* **would not** *want to do*, **that I do.**

20. **Now if I** *actually* **do that** *which* **I** *profess that I* **would not** *want to do*, **it is no more I that do it, but**, *in truth, the power of* **sin that** *still* **dwelleth** *with*in **me.**

21. **I find then a**n *operating* **law, that, when I would** *want to* **do good, evil is** *currently* **present with me.**

22.   For I *profess that I* delight in the law of God, after the inward man.

23.   But *in reality*, I see another law *operating with*in my members, *(that is, the Law of the Flesh)*, warring against the Law of my Mind, and bringing me into *the* captivity to the Law of Sin which is *operating* in *and affecting* my *bodily* members.

24.   O wretched man that I am! Who shall *be able to* deliver me from the body of this *spiritual* death?

25.   I thank God *for the New Birth that he has made available* through Jesus Christ our Lord. So then with the mind *portion of my soul*, I myself serve the law of God; but with the flesh *portion of my being*, the Law of Sin.

CHAPTER 8

1.   *There is* therefore now, *after the reality of resurrection redemption*, no *more* condemnation to them which are *now Born-Again, and* in Christ Jesus, who *regularly* walk not after the *dictates of the* flesh, but after the *leading of their newly Born-Again, recreated, Human* spirit.

2.   For the *brand-new* law of the *Holy* Spirit *of God*, *by the name* of **Life in Christ Jesus,** hath made me free from the *existing* **Law of Sin** and *the condition of* death *that goes with it.*

3.   For what the Law *of Moses* could not do, in that it was weak through the *natural* flesh, God sending his own Son in the *outward* likeness of sinful flesh, and for *the purpose of definitively dealing with* sin, condemned *the Law of* Sin in the flesh, *in the person of Jesus Christ.*

4.   That the *legal* righteousness *that is* of the Law *of Moses* might be fulfilled in *each one of* us, who walk not after the *dictates of the* flesh, but after the *leading of the newly, Born-Again, recreated, Human* spirit.

5.   For they that are *running* after the *dictates of the* flesh do *pay attention to and* mind the things of the flesh. But they that are *seeking* after the *growth and development of the newly, Born-Again, recreated, Human* spirit, *they shall mind* the things of the Spirit.

6.   For to *continue to* be carnally minded *is going to result in* death. But *purposing* to be*come* spiritually minded, *by the renewing of our mind on the word of God,* **is** *going to result in* life and peace.

7.   Because the carnal mind *of any man, redeemed or unredeemed,* **is** enmity against God. For it is not *willingly* subject to the law of God, neither indeed can *it* be, *because of its continued servitude to sin.*

8.   So then they that are *carnally minded, whether they are redeemed or unredeemed, and are being compelled by sin, to continue to walk* in the *natural* flesh, cannot please God.

9.   But ye are not *compelled to walk* in the *natural* flesh, but *rather to walk* in the *Born-Again, recreated, Human* spirit, if so be that the Spirit of God dwell in you *and your mind is being renewed by the word of God.* Now if any man *throughout the whole of the world* have not the *recreative* Spirit of Christ *living within him*, he is *not saved from damnation, and he is* none of his.

10.   And if Christ *truly be* in you, *then* the *physical* body *is technically and morally* dead because of sin; but the *newly Born-Again, recreated, Human* spirit is *full of* life because of *the* righteousness *of God that exists by being in Christ Jesus.*

11.   But if the *Holy* Spirit of him, *that is, God the Father,* that raised up *Christ* Jesus from the dead *shall* dwell *and reside* in you, *then* he that raised up Christ *Jesus* from the dead, shall also *be able to* quicken *and heal* your mortal bodies by his *Holy* Spirit that dwelleth in you.

12.   Therefore, *my* brethren, we are debtors not, to the flesh *in any way*, to *have to continue to* live after the flesh.

13.   For if ye *choose to continue to* live after the flesh, ye shall *eventually, spiritually* die *once again.* *(Jude 12)* But if ye, through the *help of the Holy* Spirit, do mortify *and put to death,* the *evil* deeds of the *physical* body, *and the unrenewed mind,* ye shall live *for evermore.*

14.   For as many as are *choosing to be* led by the *Holy* Spirit of God, *as he directs the newly Born-Again, recreated, Human spirit,* they are the sons of God.

15.   For ye have not received the *evil* spirit of bondage again *which leads you* to fear. But ye have received the *ministration and indwelling of the* Spirit of Adoption, *which is the Holy Spirit,* whereby we *are able to legally* cry *out,* Abba, Father.

16.   The *Holy* Spirit itself *being able to* beareth witness with our *own Born-Again, recreated, Human* spirit, that we are *now indeed* the children of *the Most High* God.

17.   And if *legitimate* children *of God,* then heirs *of all that he owns.* Heirs of God, and joint-heirs with Christ *Jesus our brother.* If so be that we suffer with *him as he suffered,* that we may be also glorified together *with him when the time comes.*

18.   For I *personally* reckon that the sufferings of this present time *are* not *even* worthy to be *compared* with the *magnificent* glory which shall be revealed in us *at his coming.*

19.   For the earnest expectation of the *created* creature *known of as Mankind (i.e. Humanity),* waiteth for the *soon coming* manifestation of the *actual, newly* birthed sons of God, *when they finally rise up and take their place.*

20. For the *created* **creature** *of Mankind,* **was made subject to vanity** *because of the power of sin,* **not willingly** *as a whole,* **but by reason of him who** *through his foreknowledge* **hath** *allowed this* **subject***ion,* **in** *the* **hope** *of the family that he would ultimately obtain.*

21. **Because the** *created* **creature** *of Mankind* **itself, also shall be delivered from the bondage of** *sin's* **corruption,** *when the purification of "renovation by fire" (II Peter 3:10) occurs, and they step* **into the glorious liberty of the** *actual Born-Again* **children of God.**

22. **For we know that the whole of** *the created* **creation** *of Mankind* **groaneth and travaileth in pain together***, because of sin's consequences,* **until now.**

23. **And not only** *they* *of this world,* **but** *we* **ourselves also, which have the firstfruits***, or the down payment,* **of the** *Holy* **Spirit. Even we ourselves, groan within ourselves, waiting for the adoption** *finalization,* **to wit, the redemption of our** *physical* **body** *transitioning into our promised spiritual body.*

24. **For we are** *technically* **saved by hope. But hope that is** *actually* **seen, is not** *really* **hope. For what a man** *is actually able to* **seeth** *with his own eyes; then* **why doth he yet** *need to* **hope for** *it?*

25. **But if we hope for that** *which* **we see not,** *then* **do we with patience wait for it.**

26. **Likewise, the** *Holy* **Spirit** *of God* **also helpeth our infirmities. For** *oftentimes* **we know not what we**

should pray for as we ought *to*. But the *Holy* Spirit itself, maketh intercession for us with groanings *from unknown tongues*, which *usually* cannot be uttered *and understood on this earth.*

27.   And he that searcheth the hearts *of men, which indeed the Lord Jesus does*, knoweth what *is* the mind of the *Holy* Spirit, because he *is the one who* maketh intercession for *all of* the saints according to *the will* of God *the Father.*

28.   And we *should* know that all things *ultimately* work for good, to them that love God, to them who are *indeed* **the called** according to *his* purpose.

29.   For whom he did foreknow, *from before the foundation of the world*, he also did predestinate, *within the planned finished work of the cross*, to be *precisely* conformed to the *very* image of his *Only Begotten* Son, that he might be the firstborn among many brethren, *who shall ultimately think like he thinks, and talk like he talks, and act like he acts.*

30.   Moreover, whom he did predestinate, *through the redemptive plan*, them he also called *to be his own*, and whom he called *to be his own*, them he also justified *from their transgression and sin*. And whom he justified *from their transgression and sin*, them he also glorified, *just as he glorified his Only Begotten.*

31.　*So,* **what shall we then say to these things? If God be for us,** *and on our side,* **who** *can be* **against us,** *and prevail in any area?*

32.　**He that spared not his own** *anointed* **Son, but** *willingly* **delivered him up** *to the powers of darkness, as a sacrifice* **for us all, how shall he not with him***, and his explosive resurrection power,* **also freely give** *unto* **us all things?**

33.　**Who shall** *be able to* **lay any thing to the charge of God's elect***ed children?* ***It is*** *the Almighty* **God that justifieth***by faith, and forgives to the uttermost.*

34.　**Who is he that** *is able to* **condemneth?** ***It is*** **Christ** *Jesus* **that died** *for sin,* **yea rather, that is risen** *unto life* **again,** *and* **who also** *continues to* **maketh intercession for us.**

35.　**Who shall separate us from the** *unchanging* **love of Christ?** ***Shall*** *persistent* **tribulation, or** *unpleasant* **distress, or** *evil* **persecution, or** *a* **famine** *from sustenance,* **or** *a* **nakedness** *of the body,* **or** *dangerous* **peril, or** *a threat of the* **sword?**

36.　**As it is written, "For thy sake we are killed all the day long; we are accounted as sheep for the slaughter."** *(Psalms 44:22)*

37.　**Nay, in all** *of* **these things we are** *much* **more than conquerors through him that loved us.**

38.　**For I am** *fully* **persuaded, that neither** *threat of* **death, nor** *abundance of* **life, nor** *holy or unholy* **angels,** nor *reigning* principalities, nor *demonstrated* powers, nor things *currently* present, nor things *potentially* to come,

39.　　Nor *exalted* height, nor *plunging* depth, nor any **Other Creature** *of a moral constituency*, shall be able to separate us from the *unchanging* love of God, which is *found resident with*in Christ Jesus our Lord.

CHAPTER 9

1.　　I say *unto you* the truth in Christ, *and* I lie not, my conscience also bearing me witness in the Holy Ghost,

2.　　That I have *a* great heaviness and *a* continual sorrow in my heart.

3.　　For I could *only* wish that *I* myself were accursed from Christ, *in an exchange* for my *own* brethren, my *beloved* kinsmen according to the flesh.

4.　　Who are *indeed* Israelites. *And,* to whom **pertaineth** the *pre-planned* adoption, and the *extended* glory *of God*, and the *original* covenants, and the giving of the Law *of Moses for the purpose of behavioral modification*, and the *various* services **of God**, and the *marvelous* promises *of redemption and inheritance*.

5.　　Whose **are** *indeed* the *patriarch* fathers, and of whom as concerning the *natural* flesh Christ *came*, who is over all, God blessed for ever. Amen.

6.   Not as though the word of God hath taken none effect, *because of those unconverted Jewish individuals who have refused the provision.* For they *are* not all *going to be counted as being part of* Israel, which are *simply* of *the natural Nation of* Israel.

7.   Neither, *just* because they are the *natural* seed of Abraham, *are they* all *recognized as being* children. But, *as it is prophetically written,* "In *thy promised son* Isaac shall thy seed be called." *(Genesis 21:12)*

8.   That is, they which are *just* the children of the *natural* flesh, these *are* not the *ones who shall become the* children of *the Most High* God. But the children of the promise, *which is found within Christ Jesus,* are counted for the seed.

9.   For this *is* the word of promise, "At this time will I come, and Sarah shall have a son." *(Genesis 18:10)*

10.   And not only *this fulfillment of a promise*; but when *precious* Rebecca also had conceived by one, *even* by our father Isaac, *who was the child of a "promise"*:

11.   (For *the children*, being not yet *even* born, neither having done any good or evil, that the *divine* purpose of God according to "election" might stand, *and have validity*; not of *Human* works, but of him that *purposes to* calleth;)

12.   It was said unto her, "The elder *of the two* shall serve the younger *of the two*." *(Genesis 25:23)*

13.   As it is written, "Jacob have I loved, but Esau have I hated." *(Malachi 1:1-3)*

14.   What shall we say then? *Is there* unrighteousness with God, *in how he hath prepared the redemption plan?* God forbid!

15.   For he saith to Moses, "I will have mercy on whom I will have mercy, and I will have compassion on whom I will have compassion." *(Exodus 33:19)*

16.   So then *it is* not *established simply* of him that willeth, nor of him that runneth, but *it is established* of God, that sheweth mercy *unto whom he will.*

17.   For the Scripture saith unto Pharaoh, "Even for this same purpose have I raised thee up, that I might shew my power in thee, and that my name might be declared throughout all *of* the earth." *(Exodus 9:16)*

18.   Therefore, hath he mercy on whom he will *have mercy*, and whom he will he hardeneth.

19.   Thou wilt say then unto me, Why doth he yet find fault? For who hath resisted his will?

20.   Nay but, O man, who *dost thou think that thou art* . . . thou that repliest against God? Shall the thing *that is* formed say to him that formed *it*, Why hast thou made me thus?

21.   Hath not the *creative* potter, power over the clay, of the same *muddy* lump, to make one vessel unto honour, and another *vessel* unto dishonor?

22.   *What* if God, *in* willing to shew *his* wrath, and to make his power known, endured with much longsuffering the vessels of wrath fitted *un*to destruction.

23.   And, that he might make known *unto all,* the riches of his glory *manifested* on the vessels of mercy, which he had afore prepared unto glory.

24.   Even *unto* us, whom he hath called *according to his purpose,* not of the *circumcision* Jews only, but also of the *heathen* Gentiles?

25.   As he saith also in O-see, "I will call them my *own* people, which were not *originally* my people; and her beloved, which was not beloved." *(Hosea 2:23)*

26.   And it shall *surely* come to pass, *that* in the *very* place where it was said unto them, "Ye *are* not my people"; there shall they be called the *adopted* children of the living God. *(Hosea 1:9-10)*

27.   Esaias also crieth concerning *the Nation of* Israel, "Though the number of the *natural* children of Israel be as the sand of the sea, *only* a remnant shall be saved *from destruction.*" *(Isaiah 10:22-23)*

28.   For he will finish the *pre-determined* work, and cut *it* short in righteousness: because a short *probational* work will the Lord make upon the earth.

29.   And as Esaias said before, "Except the Lord of Sabaoth had left *unto* us a seed, we *would*

had been as *the city of* Sodoma, and been made like unto Gomorrah." *(Isaiah 1:9)*

30.   What shall we say then *to these things*? That the *heathen, pagan, uncircumcised* Gentiles, which followed not after righteousness, have *now* attained *un*to righteousness, even the *very* righteousness which is of faith.

31.   But Israel, which *thought that they* followed after the law of righteousness *through adherence to the Mosaic Law,* hath not attained to the law of righteousness.

32.   Wherefore? Because *they sought it* not by faith, but as it were by *attempting to please God through* the works of the law. For they stumbled at that stumblingstone.

33.   As it is written, "Behold, I lay in Sion a stumblingstone and a rock of offence. And whosoever believeth on him shall not be ashamed." *(Isaiah 8:14)*

CHAPTER 10

1.   Brethren, my heart's *cry, and* desire and prayer to God for Israel is, that they might be saved *from spiritual death and eternal damnation.*

2.   For I *truly* bear them record that they have a *genuine* zeal of God, but not according to *Biblical, prophetical,* knowledge.

3.   For they, *regardless of what they say,* **being igno-rant of God's righteousness,** *from God's perspective and not theirs,* **and going about to establish their own righteousness,** *by their insistence of obeying the Mosaic Law,* **have** *ultimately* **not** *surrendered and* **submitted themselves unto the righteousness of God,** *which comes by demonstrated faith in the finished work of the cross of the Lord Jesus Christ.*

4.   **For Christ** *Jesus* **is the end of the law of righteousness,** *in total,* **to every one that** *chooses to* **believeth.**

5.   **For Moses describeth** *clearly* **the righteous-ness which is** *potentially obtainable* **of the Law** *of Moses,* **"That the man which doeth those things** *that the Law demands,* **shall** *then* **live** *completely* **by them,** *and not be able to pick and choose which part of the Law that he wants to obey or disobey." (Leviticus 18:5)*

6.   **But the righteousness which is** *only* **of faith, speaketh on this wise, Say not in thine heart, "Who shall ascend into** *the* **heaven? (that is, to bring Christ,** *the anointed One,* **down** *from above***.)**

7.   **Or, Who shall descend into the deep? (that is, to bring up Christ,** *the anointed One,* **again from the** *crucified* **dead.)"** *(Deuteronomy 30:12-13)*

8.   **But what saith it? "The word** *of redemption* **is nigh thee,** *even* **in thy mouth, and in thy heart."**

(Deuteronomy 30:14) That is, the word of faith *in Christ alone*, which we preach.

9.   *So* that if thou shalt confess with *the words of* thy mouth the Lord Jesus, and shalt *truly* believe in thine heart that God hath raised him *up* from the dead *again*, thou shalt be saved.

10.   For with*in* the *very* heart, *a* man *can* believeth unto righteousness; and *then, because of the abundance of what is now in the heart,* with the *words of thy* mouth, confession is made unto salvation.

11.   For the Scripture saith, "Whosoever believeth on him shall not be ashamed." *(Isaiah 28:16 & 49:23)*

12.   For there is no difference *with God* between the *natural, unconverted, Abrahamic Covenant* Jew and the *heathen, pagan, natural, unconverted, uncircumcised* Greek. For the same Lord *that is* over all *Human Beings,* is rich unto all *Human Beings* that call upon him.

13.   For whosoever *from amongst Humanity, that* shall call upon the name of the Lord *in faith,* shall be saved.

14.   How then shall they call *up*on him, in whom they have not *yet* believed? And how shall they *yet* believe in him, of whom they have not *even* heard? And how shall they *ever* hear, without a preacher *ministering the word of truth?*

15.   And how shall they *go forth and* preach, except they be *commissioned and* sent? As it is written, "How beautiful are the feet of them that preach the Gospel of Peace, and bring glad tidings of good things *from God*!" *(Isaiah 52:7)*

16.   But they *which have heard,* have not all obeyed the gospel. For Esaias saith, "Lord, who hath believed our report?" *(Isaiah 53:1)*

17.   So then faith *cometh* by hearing *from God,* and hearing *from God,* by the word of God.

18.   But I say, Have they not *all* heard? Yes verily, their sound went into all *of* the *known* earth, and their words unto the ends of the world.

19.   But I say, Did not Israel know *of the salvation that was to come by "the Christ"*? First Moses saith, "I will provoke you *un*to jealousy by *them that are* no people, *and* by a foolish nation I will anger you." *(Deuteronomy 32:21)*

20.   But Esaias is very bold, and saith, "I was found of them that sought me not; I was made manifest unto them that asked not after me." *(Isaiah 65:1-2)*

21.   But *un*to Israel he saith, "All day long I have stretched forth my hands *patiently* unto a *continually* disobedient and gainsaying people."

CHAPTER 11

1.   I say then, Hath God *really* cast away his *Covenant Chosen* **People,** *because of their stiffneckedness?* **God forbid! For I also am an Israelite,** *who am a descendant* **of the seed of Abraham,** *specifically* **of the tribe of Benjamin.**

2.   *And I declare that,* **God hath not cast away his people which he foreknew. Wot ye not what the Scripture saith of** *the prophet* **Elias,** *who is Elijah?* **How he maketh** *a prayer of* **intercession** *un*to **God against Israel, saying,**

3.   **"Lord, they have killed thy** *other* **prophets, and** *have* **digged down thine** *sacred* **altars; and I am left alone, and** *now,* **they seek my life."** *(I Kings 19:10 18)*

4.   **But what saith the answer of God unto him?** *"Fear not, for* **I have reserved** *un*to **myself** *even* **seven thousand men, who have not bowed the knee to** *the image* **of Baal."** *(I Kings 19:18)*

5.   **Even so then** *now,* **at this present time also, there is a remnant** *of covenant men,* **according to the** *purpose of the* **election of grace.**

6.   **And if by** *unmerited* **grace, then** *is it* **no more** *actually* **of works: otherwise** *unmerited* **grace is no more grace. But,** *on the other hand,* **if** *it be* **of works, then is it** *really* **no more** *of unmerited* **grace: otherwise** *the* **work is no more** *considered* **work?**

7.   What then *is the conclusion? The Nation of* Israel hath not obtained *unto* that which he seeketh for; but *those who willingly received of* the election *of extended grace* hath *indeed* obtained it, and the rest *of the nation* were blinded.

8.   (According as it is written, "God hath given *unto* them the spirit of slumber, *that is,* eyes that they should not see, and ears that they should not hear;)" *even* unto this day. *(Isaiah 29:10)*

9.   And *the Psalmist* David saith, "Let their *offering* table be made a snare, and a trap, and a stumblingblock, and a recompence unto them:

10.   Let their eyes be darkened *with spiritual blindness*, that they may not *truly* see, and *so continue to* bow down their back always." *(Psalms 69:22-23)*

11.   I say then, Have they *intentionally* stumbled that they should fall? God forbid! But *rather* through their fall*, even as the Scriptures foretold of,* salvation *is now* be*come available* unto the *heathen, pagan, unredeemed,* Gentiles, for *the prophetical purpose of the plan of God,* to provoke them *un*to jealousy.

12.   Now if the fall*ing away* of them *becomes* the riches of the world, and the diminishing of them *becomes* the riches of the *uncircumcised* Gentiles; how much more *then shall be* their fulness?

13.   For I speak *un*to you Gentiles, inasmuch as I am *commissioned by Jesus Christ himself, as* the apostle of the Gentiles, I magnify mine office.

14.   If by *doing so, by* any means I may provoke to emulation **them which are** *of* my *natural* flesh, and might *perchance* save some of them.

15.   For if the casting away of them*, which remain natural and unconverted, into a spiritual suspension,* **be** the reconciling of the *entire* world *unto God, then* what **shall** the receiving **of them** *into the finished work of the cross* **be,** but *glorious spiritual* life from the dead?

16.   For if the firstfruit*(of spiritual New-Life), which is "the Christ"* be holy, *then* the *very* lump *from which "the Christ" emanated forth from* is also *counted as* **holy.** And if the root *of the given plant* **bc** holy, *then* so **are** the branches *that emanate forth from that same root.*

17.   And if some of the *natural* branches be broken off, *because of unbelief,* and thou, being *come from* a wild *covenant-less* olive tree, wert grafted in among them *because of extended grace*, and with them *thou* partakes of the *Life from the* root and *the* fatness of the *natural covenant* olive tree;

18.   Boast not against the branches *that were broken off.* But if thou *choose to* boast, *just remember that* thou bearest not the *holy* root, but the *firstfruit, holy* root *bearest* thee.

19.   Thou wilt say then, The branches were broken off *by God,* that I might be grafted in *instead.*

20.   Well, *it was* because of *the sin of* unbelief *that* they were broken off, *just as in the Old Testament, when the Nation of Israel could not enter into the promised land because of unbelief. (Hebrews 3:19)* And thou standest by faith *today.* But, be not highminded *against the chosen of God,* but fear;

21.   For if God spared not the natural branches *of his covenant nation,* **take heed** lest he also spare not thee.

22.   Behold therefore the goodness and severity of God. On them which fell *because of their unbelief,* severity; but toward thee *that believeth,* goodness, if thou continue *by faith* in **his** goodness: otherwise thou also shalt be *summarily* cut off.

23.   And they also, if they *choose to* abide not still in *their* unbelief, shall be grafted in *once more.* For God is able to graft them in again.

24.   For if thou wert *originally* cut out of the *covenant-less* olive tree, which is wild by *its very* nature, and wert grafted *in,* contrary to *that wild* nature, into a good olive tree: *then* how much more shall these, which *already* be the natural *covenant* **branches,** be *able to be* grafted in *again* to their own olive tree?

25.   For I would not, brethren, that ye should be *spiritually* ignorant of this mystery, lest ye should be*come* wise in your own conceits; that *spiritual* blindness, *at least* in part, is happened *un*to *the Nation of* Israel, until the *Biblical* "fulness of the Gentiles" be come in, *during the Church Age.*

26.   And so, *at the time of the Second Coming of Christ,* all *of the remnant of the Nation of* Israel shall be saved *from being destroyed by the Antichrist.* As it is written, "There shall come out of Sion the Deliverer, and shall turn away ungodliness from Jacob.

27.   For this is my covenant unto them, when I shall take away their sins." *(Isaiah 27:9 & 59:20-21)*

28.   As concerning the *current preaching of the* gospel, *they are* enemies *of the gospel* for your sakes. But as touching the election *of God*, they are *truly* beloved for the *patriarch* father's sakes.

29.   For the *granted* gifts and *the* calling of God *are* without repentance.

30.   For as ye *Gentiles*, in times past, have not believed *in the One True* God, yet have now obtained mercy *because of, and* through, their unbelief.

31.   Even so have these *chosen, Abrahamic Covenant people*, also now not believed *just like you*, that through your *demonstrated* mercy *and love*, they also may obtain mercy *through the goodness of God.*

32.   For God hath concluded them all, *both Jew and Gentile alike*, in unbelief, that he might have

mercy upon all *who would surrender, to the finished work of Christ Jesus upon the cross of Calvary.*

33.   O the depth of the riches, both of the wisdom and *the* knowledge of God! How unsearchable *are* his judgments, and his *intricate* ways past finding out!

34.   For who*, amongst Mankind,* hath known the mind of the Lord? Or who hath been *qualified to be* his counsellor?

35.   Or who hath *taken the initiative and* first given *un*to him, and *then* it shall be recompensed *back* unto him again?

36.   For of him *alone,* and through him *alone,* and *un*to him *alone, are* all things: to whom *be the* glory for ever. Amen.

CHAPTER 12

1.   I beseech *and plead with* you therefore, *my beloved* brethren, by the mercies of *a loving* God, that *now, as a declared priest of God,* ye present your *physical* bodies *as* a living sacrifice, holy, acceptable unto God, which is your reasonable service, *and the least that you can do.*

2.   And be *ye* not conformed *un*to this *carnal* world *system*: but *rather,* be ye *raised above this world, and* transformed *into the New Creation individual that Christ*

has made you to be, by the renewing of your mind. That ye may *now* prove what *is* that good *aspect,* and *that* acceptable *aspect,* and *that* perfect *aspect, of the one* will of *the living* God.

3.   For I say *unto you, by the Holy Spirit,* through the grace *that is* given unto me, to every *single* man that is among you, not to *pridefully* think *of himself* more highly than he ought to think. But to think soberly, according as God hath dealt to every *individual* man "the" measure of faith.

4.   For as we have many *different* members *operating with*in *our personal* one body, and all *of those* members have not the same office, *nor do the very same thing*:

5.   So we, *being* many *members in particular,* are *just* one body in Christ, and every one *of us* members one of another.

6.   Having then *spiritual, motivational* gift*ing*s, differing according to the *extended* grace that is given *un*to us; whether *the gift of* prophecy, *let us prophesy* according to the proportion of *the* faith *that we have developed through the word of God.*

7.   Or *a gift of* ministry *and serving other persons,* **let us wait** *on the direction of the Holy Spirit* **on** *how and where* **our** ministering *or serving should take place.* **Or he that** *is called to* teacheth, **on** *how and what and where he should be* teaching.

8.   Or he that *is gifted to* exhorteth, on *whom should receive the* exhortation. He that giveth *from a cheerful heart,* let *him do it* with simplicity. He that *administrates and* ruleth, *carefully doing so* with diligence *and wisdom. And,* he that sheweth mercy *unto him that is in need, doing so* with cheerfulness.

9.   *Let genuine* love be without dissimulation. Abhor that which is evil *even as God abhors evil.* Cleave *un*to that which is good *and proper.*

10.   *Be* kindly affectioned one to another with *sincere* brotherly love; in *deserved* honour preferring one another.

11.   Not *being* slothful in business *affairs, but* fervent in spirit, *always* serving the Lord.

12.   Rejoicing in *the* hope *that we have in Christ.* Patient in *various kinds of* tribulation. *And,* continuing instant in prayer, *in season and out of season.*

13.   Distributing to the necessity of *the household of the* saints. Given *un*to hospitality *and graciousness.*

14.   Bless them which *come against you and* persecute you. Bless *them,* and curse *them* not.

15.   Rejoice with them that do rejoice, and weep with them that *do* weep.

16.   *Be* of the same mind one toward another. Mind not *the* high things *of this world,* but condescend to men of low estate. Be not wise in your own *personal* conceits.

17.   Recompense *un*to no man evil for *the* evil *that he has done unto you.* Provide *for* things *that are* honest in the sight of all men; *whether they be redeemed or unredeemed.*

18.   If it be possible, *for* as much as lieth in you, *purpose to* live peaceably with all men.

19.   Dearly beloved, avenge not yourselves *upon others*, but **rather** give place unto wrath. For it is written, "Vengeance is mine; I will repay, saith the Lord." *(Deuteronomy 32:35-36)*

20.   Therefore if thine enemy hunger, *extend to him the love of God and* feed him. If he thirst, *be gracious to* give him *a* drink. For in so doing thou shalt heap *invisible* coals of fire *and guilt up*on his head.

21.   Be not overcome of evil, but *rather,* overcome evil with good.

CHAPTER 13

1.   Let every *New Creation* soul be subject unto the higher powers *of a beneficent government or administration.* For there is no *beneficent* power but *that which is* of God. The *beneficent* powers that be *in place now* are ordained of God.

2.   Whosoever therefore *that* resisteth the power *of a beneficent government of administration,* resisteth the

very ordinance of God. And they that *choose to* resist shall *ultimately* receive *un*to themselves damnation.

3.   For *beneficent* rulers are not a terror *un*to *those individuals who do* good works, but *they are un*to the *individuals that doeth* evil *works.* Wilt thou then*, as a New Creature,* not be afraid of the power *of a beneficent government or administration?* *In practicality,* do that which is good, and thou shalt have praise of the same.

4.   For he is the minister *and servant* of God *un*to thee for *thy* good. But if thou *choose to* do that which is evil be afraid. For he beareth not the *legal* sword in vain. For he is the minister *and servant* of God *himself,* a revenger *of righteousness,* to **execute** *deserved* wrath upon him that doeth evil.

5.   Wherefore *ye* must needs be subject *as a New Creature,* not only for wrath, but also for con- science sake.

6.   For *it is* for this cause *that ye should* pay ye tribute also. For they *also* are God's *servant* minis- ters, attending continually upon this very thing.

7.   Render therefore to all *that are approved,* their *required* dues: Tribute *un*to whom tribute *is due;* custom *un*to whom custom *is due; godly* fear *un*to whom *godly* fear *is due; and* honour *un*to whom hon- our *is due.*

8.   Owe no man any thing, but to love one another. For he that loveth another hath fulfilled the
Royal Law.

9.   For this, "Thou shalt not commit adultery,
Thou shalt not kill, Thou shalt not steal, Thou
shalt not bear false witness, Thou shalt not covet;"
and if *there be* any other *Mosaic Law* commandment, it is briefly comprehended in this
saying, namely, "Thou shalt love thy neighbor as
thyself."

10.   *Genuine* love worketh no ill to*ward* his neighbor. Therefore love is the fulfilling of the *Royal*
Law, *that Jesus himself established.*

11.   And that, knowing the *shortness of the* time,
that now *it is* high time to awake out of *our* sleep.
For now *is* our salvation *much* nearer than when we
first believed.

12.   The night is *already* far spent, *and* the day is
at hand. Let us therefore cast off the *unfruitful*
works of darkness, and let us put on the *protective*
armour of light.

13.   Let us *truly* walk honestly, as in the day. Not
in rioting and drunkenness, not in chambering
and wantonness, not in strife and envying.

14.   But *actively* put ye on the Lord Jesus Christ,
and make not *any* provision for the flesh, to *fulfil*
the *vile* lusts *thereof.*

CHAPTER 14

1. Him that is weak in the *walk of* faith receive ye, *but* not to *striving,* doubtful disputations.
2. For one *man* believeth that he may eat *of* all things. Another *man*, who is weak, eateth *only* herbs.
3. Let not him that eateth *all things,* despise him that eateth not *but herbs.* And let not him which eateth not *begin to* judge him that eateth: for God hath received him.
4. Who art thou that *presumeth to* judgest another man's servant? To his own master he *is able to* standeth or falleth. Yea, he shall be holden up: for God is able to make him stand.
5. One man esteemeth one day above another *for the purpose of worship*: *and* another esteemeth every day *alike.* Let every man be fully persuaded in his own mind.
6. He that regardeth the *Sabbath of commandment* day, *in order to worship God,* regardeth *it as a day dedicated* unto the Lord. And he that regardeth not the *Sabbath of commandment* day *as the dedicated day of worship*, to the Lord he doth not regard it. He that eateth, *whether it be all things, or only herbs*, eateth *un*to the Lord, for he giveth *unto the* God *of his provision,* thanks. And he that eateth not *of all things*, to the

Lord he eateth not, and *also* giveth God thanks *for his provision.*

7.   For none of us liveth *only un*to himself, and no man dieth *only un*to himself.

8.   For whether we *continue to* live, we live unto the Lord; and whether we die, we die unto the Lord. Whether we live therefore, or die, we are the Lord's.

9.   For to this end Christ both died *spiritually and physically,* and rose *both spiritually and physically,* and revived *those who had died afore time,* that he might be Lord both of the dead and *of the* living.

10.   But why dost thou *choose to* judge thy brother? Or why dost thou *purpose to* set at nought thy brother? For we shall all stand before the *Bema* judgment seat of Christ.

11.   For it is written, "As I live, saith the Lord, every knee shall bow to me, and every tongue shall confess to God." *(Isaiah 45:23)*

12.   So then every *single* one of us shall give *an* account of himself to *the Second Person of the* **God**head, *even Jesus, concerning the deeds done in the body, whether they be good or evil.*

13.   Let us not therefore *prematurely* judge one another any more. But judge this rather, that no man put a stumblingblock or an occasion *for one* to fall in *his* brother's way.

14. I *personally* know, and am persuaded by the Lord Jesus, that *there is* nothing *that is* unclean *in and* of itself. But to him that esteemeth any thing to be unclean, *then* to him *it really is* unclean.

15. But if thy brother *in Christ* be grieved with *thy* meat, *because of his weakness*, now walkest thou not charitably, *because thou should knowest better.*

16. Let not then your good *intention be misunderstood, and* be evil spoken of.

17. For the kingdom of *our* God is not *founded in physical elements such as* meat and drink; but *the kingdom of our God finds its foundation in* righteousness, and peace, and *in* joy in the Holy Ghost.

18. For he, that in these *spiritual* things serveth Christ, *is* acceptable *un*to God, and approved of men.

19. Let us therefore *purpose to* follow after the things which make for peace, and things wherewith one *saint* may edify another.

20. For *various physical* meat destroy*s* not the work*ings* of God. All things indeed *are* pure *unto he who is pure*; but *it is* evil *entreated* for that man who *chooseth to* eateth with offence.

21. *It is a* good *thing* neither to eat flesh, nor to drink wine, nor *to do* **any thing** *else* whereby thy brother stumbleth, or is offended, or is made weak.

22.   Hast thou faith *as thou proclaims*? Have *it unto* thyself before God. Happy *is* he that condemneth not himself, in that *very* thing which he alloweth *in others*.

23.   And he that *wavereth and* doubteth is damned if he *goeth ahead and* eat*eth*, because *he eateth* not of faith. For *in our walk with our New Creation Lord Jesus Christ*, whatsoever *is* not of faith is sin.

CHAPTER 15

1.   We then that *profess that we* are *spiritually* strong ought to bear the infirmities of the *spiritually* weak, and not *just live* to please ourselves.

2.   Let every one of us please *his* neighbor for *his benefit and* good to edification.

3.   For even Christ *Jesus* pleased not himself *while he was here on the earth*; but, as it is written, "The reproaches of them that reproached thee, fell on me." *(Psalms 69:9)*

4.   For whatsoever things were written *in the Scriptures* aforetime, were written for our learning *and spiritual education*, that we through patience and comfort of *what* the Scriptures *declare*, might have hope.

5.   Now the God of *all* patience and consolation grant *unto* you to be likeminded one toward another according to *the desire of* Christ Jesus.

6.   That ye may *all,* with one mind *and* one mouth glorify God, even the Father of our Lord Jesus Christ.

7.   Wherefore receive ye one another *without disputation,* as Christ also *fully* received us to the glory of God *the Father.*

8.   Now I say *the truth, and lie not,* that Jesus Christ was a minister of, *and to,* the *covenant* circumcision *Jewish people,* for the *demonstrated* truth of God, to confirm the *covenant* promises *that were* **made** unto the *patriarch* fathers.

9.   And that *after his death and resurrection, that* the Gentiles might glorify God for *his* *gracious* mercy; as it is written, "For this cause I will confess to thee among the Gentiles, and sing unto thy name." *(Psalms 18:49)*

10.   And again he saith, "Rejoice ye Gentiles, with his people." *(Deuteronomy 32:48)*

11.   And again, "Praise the Lord, all ye Gentiles; and laud him, all ye people." *(Psalms 117:1)*

12.   And again, Esaias saith, "There shall be a root of Jesse, and he that shall rise to reign over the Gentiles; in him shall the Gentiles trust." *(Isaiah 11:10)*

13.　Now, *may* the God of *all* hope, fill you with all joy and peace in believing, that ye may abound in hope, through the power of the Holy Ghost.

14.　And I myself also am *become* persuaded of you, my brethren, that ye also are full of goodness, filled with all knowledge, *and* able to admonish one another.

15.　Nevertheless, *my* brethren, I have *taken the opportunity, and* written the more boldly unto you in some sort, as *of* putting you in mind, because of the grace that is given to me of God.

16.　That I should *actually* be*come* the minister of Jesus Christ to *all of* the Gentiles. Ministering the gospel of *the living* God, that the offering up of the Gentles might be*come* acceptable, being sanctified *and set apart* by the Holy Ghost.

17.　I have therefore whereof I may glory through Jesus Christ in *all of* those things which pertain to God.

18.　For I will not *even* dare to speak of any of those things which Christ hath not *personally* wrought by me, to make the Gentiles *to be* obedient by word and deed,

19.　Through mighty signs and wonders, by the power of *the spiritual gifts of* the *Holy* Spirit of God. So that *starting* from Jerusalem, and *all the way* round about unto Illyricum, I have fully preached the gospel of Christ.

20.   Yea, so have I *endeavored and* strived to preach the gospel, not where Christ was *already* named, lest I should build upon another man's foundation.

21.   But as it is written, "To whom he was not spoken of, they shall see: and they that have not heard shall understand." *(Isaiah 52:15)*

22.   For which cause also I have been much hindered from coming to you.

23.   But now, *really* having no more place *of acceptance* in these parts, and having a great desire these many years to come unto you;

24.   Whensoever I *purpose to* take my journey into Spain, I will come *un*to you *first.* For I trust to see you in my journeying, and *then* to be brought on my way thitherward by your *generosity*, if first I be somewhat filled with your *company.*

25.   But *for* now, I go unto Jerusalem to minister unto the saints *of God that are there.*

26.   For it hath pleased them of Macedonia and Achaia to make a certain *financial* contribution for the poor *circumcised, New Creation* saints, which are at Jerusalem.

27.   It hath *indeed* pleased them verily; and their debtors they *truly* are. For if the *heathen, pagan,* Gen-

tiles have been made *fellow* partakers of their spiritual things, their *unstated* duty is also to minister *back* unto them in carnal things.

28.   When therefore I have performed this *obligation*, and have sealed *un*to them this fruit, *then* I will come by you into *the country of* Spain.

29.   And I am sure that, when I come unto you, I shall come in the fulness of the blessing of the gospel of Christ.

30.   Now I beseech you, brethren, for the Lord Jesus Christ's sake, and for the love of the *Holy* Spirit, that ye strive together *in unity* with me, in *your* prayers to God for me.

31.   That I may be delivered from them that do not believe in Judaea *concerning the finished work of the cross of Christ*. And *additionally*, that my service which *I have* for Jerusalem may be *freely* accepted of the saints.

32.   That *when I come,* I may come unto you with *great* joy by the will of God, and may *along* with you be refreshed.

33.   Now the God of peace *and grace* be with you all. Amen.

CHAPTER 16

1.   I commend unto you Phebe our sister, which is a servant of *God, ministering at* the church which is at Cenchrea.

2.   *I exhort you,* that ye receive her in the Lord, as becometh saints, and that ye *aid and* assist her in whatsoever business she *may* hath need of you. For she hath been a succourer of many *saints*, and *even* of myself also.

3.   Greet Priscilla and Aquila *who are* my helpers in Christ Jesus.

4.   Who have for my *very* life laid down their own necks. Unto whom not only *do* I give thanks, but also all the churches of the Gentiles.

5.   Likewise *greet* the church that is *currently meeting* in their house. Salute my well beloved Epaenetus, who is *blessedly* the firstfruits of Achaia unto Christ.

6.   Greet *sweet* Mary, who bestowed much labour on us.

7.   Salute Andronicus and Junia, my kinsmen, and my fellow prisoners *in Christ*, who are of note among the *other* apostles, who also were *redeemed* in Christ before me.

8.   Greet Amplias my beloved *friend* in the Lord.

9.　　Salute Urbane, *who is* our helper in Christ, and *also* Stachys my beloved.

10.　　Salute Apelles *who is* approved in Christ. Salute them *all* which are of Aristobulus' *household*.

11.　　Salute Herodion my *fellow* kinsman. Greet them that be of the *household* of Narcissus, which are in the Lord.

12.　　Salute Tryphena and Tryphosa, who *continue to* labour in the Lord. Salute the beloved Persis, which *hath* labored much in the Lord.

13.　　Salute Rufus *who is* chosen in the Lord, and his mother and mine.

14.　　Salute Asyncritus, Phlegon, Hermas, Patrobas, Hermes, and *all of* the saints which are with them.

15.　　Salute Philologus, and Julia, Nereus, and his sister, and Olympas, and all *of* the saints which are with them.

16.　　Salute one another with an holy kiss. The churches of Christ *in turn* salute you.

17.　　Now I beseech you, brethren, *to make note, and* mark them which cause divisions and offences contrary to the *sound* doctrine which ye have *already* learned *of me*; and avoid them.

18.　　For they that are such serve not our Lord Jesus Christ, *even though they use his name, and talk as though they know him. But rather, they are* but *religious, and serve only* their own belly. And by *using* good words and *uttering* fair speeches, *they* deceive the hearts of the simple.

19.   For your obedience *to the faith* is come abroad unto all *men*. I am glad therefore on your behalf. But yet, I would have you *to be* wise unto that which is good, and *remain* simple concerning evil.

20.   And the God of *mercy and* peace shall bruise Satan under your feet shortly. The grace of our Lord Jesus Christ *be* with you *always*. Amen.

21.   Timotheus my workfellow *and brother in Christ*, and Lucius, and Jason, and Sosipater, my kinsman, salute you.

22.   I Tertius, who wrote *this* epistle *down on paper*, salute*th* you in the Lord.

23.   Gaius *who is* mine host, and *indeed a host* of the whole church *at times*, saluteth you. Erastus the chamberlain of the city *also* saluteth you, and *so does* Quartus *who is truly* a brother.

24.   The *extended* grace of our Lord Jesus Christ *be* with you all. Amen.

25.   Now to him that is of *the* power to *e*stablish you according to *the truth of* my gospel, and the preaching of *the New Creation Lord* Jesus Christ, according to the *received* revelation of the mystery *of*

God, which was kept secret *ever* since the world began,

26.　　But now is made *evident and* manifest; and by the Scriptures *written* of the prophets, according to the commandment of the everlasting God *Almighty*, made known to all *of the* nations for *the purpose of* the obedience of faith:

27.　　To God only wise, *be* glory through Jesus Christ for ever. Amen.

Epilogue

This is the first Biblical work with explosive enhancement. And once again, the enhancement is not inserted in order to change the text of the King James Translation of the Bible.

It is so important that the people of God have an understanding of the doctrine of justification by faith that is being established because of the finished work of Christ Jesus upon the cross of Calvary.

Christianity must break away from centuries of tradition that is still occurring during these last days of the pre-Tribulation, falling away, spoken of in II Thessalonians 2:3 . . . if we are really going to have any significant impact upon a lost and dying world in this 21st Century.

We need to know who we are in Christ, and then purpose to rise to the occasion and engage in the spiritual warfare that is all around us.

The Book of Romans is a major doctrinal work concerning post-resurrection realities. It does not present a Jesus, plus good works, venue. It does not present a Jesus, plus various aspect of the Law of Moses, venue.

It does not present a Jesus, plus *anything*, venue. It just presents a total faith in the finished work of Christ Jesus upon Calvary's cross, venue. And we cannot add to it, nor take away from it. We can only accept and receive it, or reject it, by trying to establish our own righteousness. *(Romans 10:3)*

We really need to know what it says, and not just what we think it says, or what someone else says that it says. May the blessing of the Lord be upon you as you go forth in faith.

Maranantha!

Meet the Author

By-The-Book Ministries, Inc. began in 2001 as a teaching outreach. Rob E. Daley has been gifted by God to be able to explain biblical truths in an easy to understand manner.

Many have been blessed by his teaching style.

Rob was saved and filled with the Holy Spirit in 1978 and has been instructed by the greatest teacher of all—the Spirit of Truth Himself. Rob is an ordained minister with the Assemblies of God International Fellowship and has pastored in various churches over the past 34 years.

It is the desire of this ministry to see the body of Christ solidly taught, and grow up into the things of the Lord. Rob is available for seminars, retreats, conventions, etc.

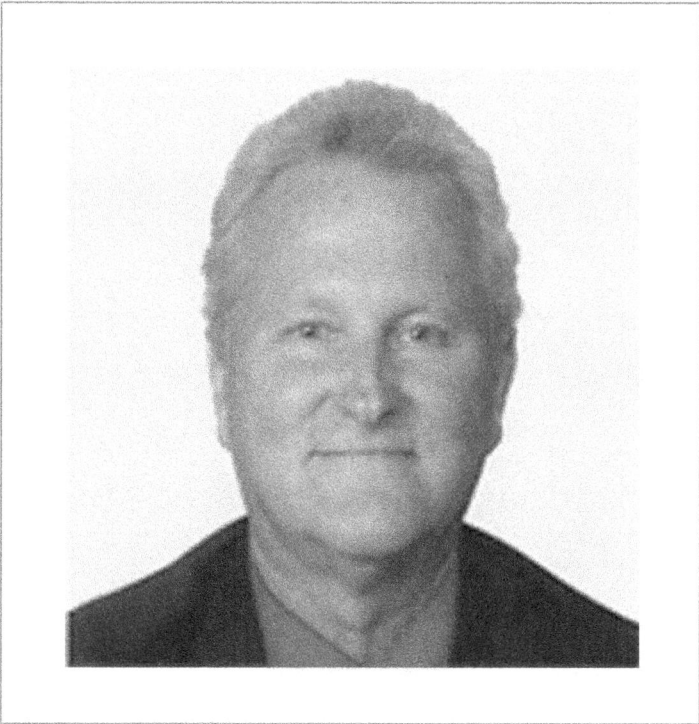

Rob can be reached at:

thedaleys@bythebookministries.org

http://robdaleyauthor.com